# Learning to read. Reading to learn!

**LEVEL ONE** Sounding It Out Preschool–Kindergarten
For kids who know their alphabet and are starting to sound out words.

learning sight words • beginning reading • sounding out words

**LEVEL TWO** Reading with Help Preschool–Grade 1
For kids who know sight words and are learning to sound out new words.

expanding vocabulary • building confidence • sounding out bigger words

**LEVEL THREE** Independent Reading Grades 1–3
For kids who are beginning to read on their own.

introducing paragraphs • challenging vocabulary • reading for comprehension

**LEVEL FOUR** Chapters Grades 2–4
For confident readers who enjoy a mixture of images and story.

reading for learning • more complex content • feeding curiosity

***Ripley Readers*** Designed to help kids build their reading skills and confidence at any level, this program offers a variety of fun, entertaining, and unbelievable topics to interest even the most reluctant readers. With stories and information that will spark their curiosity, each book will motivate them to start and keep reading.

PUBLISHING

**Vice President, Licensing & Publishing** Amanda Joiner
**Editorial Manager** Carrie Bolin

**Editor** Jordie R. Orlando
**Writer** Korynn Wible-Freels
**Designer** Mark Voss
**Reprographics** Bob Prohaska

Published by Ripley Publishing 2020

10 9 8 7 6 5 4 3 2 1

Copyright © 2020 Ripley Publishing

ISBN: 978-1-60991-343-4

For more information regarding permission, contact:
VP Licensing & Publishing
Ripley Entertainment Inc.
7576 Kingspointe Parkway, Suite 188
Orlando, Florida 32819

Email: publishing@ripleys.com
www.ripleys.com/books
Manufactured in China in January 2020.

First Printing

Library of Congress Control Number:
2019954286

PUBLISHER'S NOTE
While every effort has been made to verify the accuracy of the entries in this book, the Publisher cannot be held responsible for any errors contained in the work. They would be glad to receive any information from readers.

**PHOTO CREDITS**
**Cover** © Palto/Shutterstock.com **3** © Palto/Shutterstock.com **4** © MNStudio/Shutterstock.com **5** © A3pfamily/Shutterstock.com **6-7** © frank60/Shutterstock.com **8** © David Hicks/Shutterstock.com **10-11** © Ryan M. Bolton/Shutterstock.com **12-13** © StudioSmart/Shutterstock.com **13** (tr) © Rav Kark/Shutterstock.com **14-15** (bkg) © Daniel Eskridge/Shutterstock.com **14** © Krikkiat/Shutterstock.com **15** © Ian_Sherriffs/Shutterstock.com **16** © SemilirBanyu/Shutterstock.com **17** © eshoot/Shutterstock.com **18** © mar_chm1982/Shutterstock.com **19** © Michael Potter11/Shutterstock.com **20-21** © Shaun Jeffers/Shutterstock.com **22-23** © Elizaveta Galitckaia/Shutterstock.com **22** © Pasi Koskela/Shutterstock.com **25** © Hernando Sorzano/Shutterstock.com **26** © torook/Shutterstock.com **27** © Milan Adzic/Shutterstock.com **28** © Darkdiamond67/Shutterstock.com **29** © Matee Nuserm/Shutterstock.com **30-31** © Hurst Photo/Shutterstock.com **31** © BLUR LIFE 1975/Shutterstock.com **Master Graphics** © ShlyahovaYulia/Shutterstock.com, © Kozyreva Elena/Shutterstock.com, © Lucky Graphic/Shutterstock.com, © Kristyna Vagnerova/Shutterstock.com, © Iconikum/Shutterstock.com, © Lenin Graphics/Shutterstock.com

**Key:** t = top, b = bottom, c = center, l = left, r = right, sp = single page, dp = double page, bkg = background

# RIPLEY Readers

## Bugs!

## All true and unbelievable!

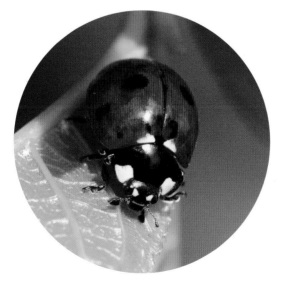

RIPLEY
PUBLISHING

a Jim Pattison Company

Do you find bugs when you play outside?

A bug is a little animal that can walk, fly, or jump!

There are a lot of different kinds!

# Did you know that ants can make a bridge?

# Ants are little but strong!

Did that stick just walk? Yes!
It is a walking stick bug!

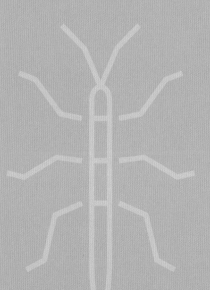

This creepy crawly is a centipede.
That name means 100 legs.

# But, they can have up to 354 legs!

Bees are helpful to the earth.

But not all bees are
yellow and black!

Picture a dragonfly
that is two feet long!

That is how big these bugs
could get in dinosaur times!

A boy praying mantis can fly, but a girl cannot.

Some look like flowers!
How pretty!

There is a beetle for every color.
Blue, white, black, yellow, and more!

What do you think
the dung beetle likes?

Poo! Yuck!

Glow worms make the cave look so pretty.

They light up the dark like glow sticks!

Slime helps the glow worms
catch bugs to eat!

Did you know mosquitos
like the smell of feet?

Put on shoes and bug spray when you go out!

All things must have air to live.

You get air with your nose, but a worm gets air with its skin!

# What is that sound?
# It is a cockroach!

The holes on its back
help it hiss!

Butterflies come from caterpillars.

They are so pretty as they fly by!

Do you like the creepy bugs or the pretty ones?

Bugs are so cool, just
as long as they are
not in the house!